# 101

# Ways to Save the
# Planet

Deborah Underwood

Chicago, Illinois

**www.capstonepub.com**
Visit our website to find out
more information about
Heinemann-Raintree books.

**To order:**
☎ Phone 800-747-4992
🖳 Visit www.capstonepub.com
to browse our catalog and order online.

Edited by Andrew Farrow and Adam Miller
Designed by Richard Parker
Picture research by Ruth Blair
Originated by Capstone Global Library Ltd
Printed in the United States of America in North
Mankato, Minnesota.   062013   007558RP

15 14 13
10 9 8 7 6 5 4 3

**Library of Congress Cataloging-in-Publication Data**
Underwood, Deborah.
 101 ways to save the planet / Deborah Underwood.
   p. cm.
 Includes bibliographical references and index.
 ISBN 978-1-4109-3898-5 (hc) -- ISBN 978-1-4109-
4385-9 (pb)
 1. Environmental protection—Juvenile literature. 2.
Conservation of natural resources—Juvenile literature.
I. Title. II. Title: One hundred one ways to save the
planet. III. Title: One hundred and one ways to save the
planet.
 TD170.15.U64 2011
  333.72—dc22      2010033924

**Acknowledgments**
We would like to thank the following for permission
to reproduce photographs: Alamy pp **37** (Andrew
Rubtsov), **46** (Bruce Coleman Inc.); Corbis pp **7** (Tim
Klein/Aurora Photos), **12** (Bloomimage), **15** (Artiga
Photo), **16** (Toby Melville/Reuters), **17** (Image Source),
**22** (Construction Photography), **29** (Randy Faris), **41**
(Ted Dayton Photography/Beateworks), **42** (Mika), **44**
(Steven Kazlowski/Science Faction), **48** (Tim Pannell),
**51** (Oliver Rossi); Getty Images p **32** (George Pimentel/
WireImage); iStockphoto pp **4** (Aldo Murillo), **21**
(Vikram Raghuvanshi Photography), **24** (Joe Potato
Photo), **34** (seraficus), **35** (Tomasz Pietryszek), **39**
(Amber Antozak), **49** (Sian Cox); Shutterstock pp
**7** (Petr Mašek), **9** (Jacob Kearns), **11 top** (Leonid
Shcheglov), **11 bottom** (Christina Richards), **13**
(LianeM), **19** (Mihai Simonia), **20** (Antonio V. Oquias),
**25** (IA98), **27** (Adrian Britton), **30** (Arvind Balaraman),
**31** (oliveromg), **33** (mikeledray), **36** (auremar), **45**
(Matsonashvili Mikhail).

Cover photograph of a teenage girl hugging a
tree, reproduced with permission of Getty Images
(Thinkstock).

Every effort has been made to contact copyright holders
of material reproduced in this book. Any omissions will
be rectified in subsequent printings if notice is given to
the publisher.

**Disclaimer**
All the Internet addresses (URLs) given in this book
were valid at the time of going to press. However, due to
the dynamic nature of the Internet, some addresses may
have changed, or sites may have changed or ceased to
exist since publication. While the author and publisher
regret any inconvenience this may cause readers, no
responsibility for any such changes can be accepted by
either the author or the publisher.

# Contents

In order to protect the privacy of individuals featured in case studies, some names have been changed.

Words appearing in the text in bold, **like this**, are explained in the Glossary.

# Introduction

We live on a pretty wonderful planet. Earth has adorable pandas, tropical islands, stunning mountains, and land to grow the food we need. Unfortunately, though, Earth also has some big problems. Even more unfortunately, these problems are our fault.

Humans have done some amazing things in the last few centuries. We have cured diseases, built computers, and harnessed the power of electricity. But in the process, we have seriously damaged our planet.

People affect the planet in many ways, both good and bad.

listen up!

Is it getting hot in here? Unfortunately, the answer is "yes." Earth's average surface temperature has increased by about 0.74 °C (1.33 °F) in the last 100 years. That's a big deal. Higher temperatures mean melting ice caps, weird weather, and rising sea levels, among other things. Scientists believe temperatures are rising because of things we humans are doing, such as burning **fossil fuels**.

### What's that?

**Fossil fuels** are materials such as oil, coal, and natural gas. They formed within Earth from the remains of plants and animals that lived millions of years ago.

## Pollution problems

Humans burn fuels and use chemicals that cause air pollution—poisonous stuff that gets into the air and harms people and other animals. Chemicals in the air also cause **acid rain**, which can harm soil, crops, and forests. It can even eat away at buildings.

# Quiz

## What does it mean when you're "green"?

a) you're very envious

b) you're very inexperienced at something

c) you're trying to help the **environment**.

### Find out the truth!

Actually, all these answers could be right. But we think the most important one is **c**. *Green* can also be used to describe environmentally friendly products, services, or businesses.

**Q** What does *eco* mean?

**A** *Eco* is a prefix that means "environmental." For example, *eco-friendly* means "environmentally friendly."

## Population growth

In 1804 the world's population was about one billion people. Now it is over six billion! That means there are six times as many people living on our planet as there were just a couple of hundred years ago.

It is the same as though there were four people living in your house, and then there were twenty-four. Do you think that might cause problems?

The world has a limited amount of some **resources**, such as oil, water, and food. As there are more people on Earth, there is also more pressure on these precious resources—and there is a greater danger of running short of these resources.

 **What's the big deal about water? You turn on the faucet and it comes out, doesn't it?**

 **Not necessarily. There are about one billion people around the world who don't have access to clean drinking water. Even those of us who are lucky enough to have it need to be careful how much of it we use. There is only a certain amount of water in the world. We need to keep it clean and use it wisely.**

# Oops!
The more people there are on the planet, the more trash we make. Some of that trash is plastic that will hang around for hundreds of years. A plastic planet is not exactly the best gift to give our great-great-great-great-grandchildren, is it?

As people spread out on the planet, there are fewer resources available for our fellow creatures. When we cut down trees to make furniture, or to free up land to grow food, we destroy other animals' **habitats**. When we pollute the oceans, the animals that live there suffer. The choices we make affect animals all over the world, from the Amazon to the Arctic. Many animal species are in danger of dying out forever because of human activities.

**listen up!**

### What's that?

A **habitat** is the place where an organism, such as an animal, lives.

## What can I do?

You can do a lot! What you do, what you eat, and what you buy can have a huge impact on the planet. You—yes, YOU!—can make the world a better place. Many environmentally friendly actions you can take will make you healthier and happier, too. You may not be able to do all these things now, but if you do even some of them, you will really be helping the planet. So roll up your sleeves and get ready to make a difference!

One person can make a big difference in the fight to save the planet.

# Eating Green

Our food choices affect a lot of things—for example, the amounts of water and fuel we use up, the amount of trash we throw away, the amount of **pesticides** we put into the soil, and how healthy we are. The good news is that making Earth-friendly food choices is an easy (and tasty) way to help the planet several times a day!

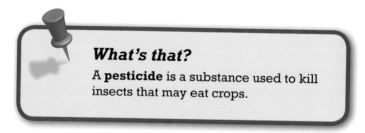

**What's that?**
A **pesticide** is a substance used to kill insects that may eat crops.

**01** Eat **organic** food when you can. Non-organic food growers may use chemicals that harm the environment.

**02** Plant a fruit and vegetable garden. Instead of driving to the supermarket and buying food that has been driven, flown, or shipped to your town, you can just go outside and pick your own.

**03** When you buy packaged food, read the label. If a food is full of chemicals you can't pronounce, you might want to think twice about eating it. It may be unhealthy, and it certainly won't be organic. Labels will also tell you if the food is organic or not.

**04** Better still, avoid packaged food whenever you can.

**05** Eat "whole foods" (see quiz on page 9). They use up less energy to produce and are usually better for you.

**06** Buy locally grown food. It takes much less fuel to transport local foods to your farmers' market or local store than to import food from other countries or states.

**07** Eat fruits and vegetables in season. If you live in a big town or city and can buy strawberries during the dead of winter, you can bet that the strawberries were grown a long way away. (Strawberries don't grow well in freezing weather!)

Look for fruits and vegetables that are organic or locally grown. Or, better yet, look for both!

# Quiz

## What is a whole food?

a) food with a hole in it, like a doughnut

b) food that you can't cut in half

c) food that is either unprocessed or has been processed very little.

### Find out the truth!

The answer is **c**. Brown rice is a whole food, because very little is done to it before it ends up on your supermarket shelf. An apple is a whole food, too, along with all whole fruits and vegetables.

But **white rice is a processed food** because the outer part of the rice has been polished away. Tomato ketchup is processed, because the tomatoes have been cooked, made into sauce, and packaged. Processing food uses energy, so eating whole foods can save energy.

## Factory farming

Today, most of the meat we buy comes from factory farms. These are places that raise huge numbers of animals in a relatively small space. Having so many animals in one place puts stress on the land. For one thing, big herds or flocks of animals make a lot of waste. Getting rid of the waste from hundreds of thousands of animals can be a big problem.

Cramming all these animals together also allows diseases to spread quickly from one animal to another. Furthermore, animals in factory farms have horrible lives. For example, chickens are often crammed together in small cages. Imagine how you would feel being trapped in a crowded elevator forever.

# Quiz

## What is a food chain?

a) a necklace made of Brussels sprouts

b) a way of showing how nutrients pass from one living thing to another

c) something you use to lock your lunchbox to your desk so no one will steal it.

### Find out the truth!

The answer is **b**. It's good to eat low on the food chain, meaning, to eat plants instead of animals. If you eat a hamburger made from a cow, you are not just eating the meat. In a way, you are also eating all the plants that the cow ever ate. You are also using up all the water that the cow drank, and all the water that it took to grow the plants the cow ate. If you only eat plants, you use up fewer resources.

These turkeys are crowded together in a factory farm. They barely have room to move.

## Where does your food come from?

There are still some smaller farms that raise animals. These farms are not as hard on the planet as factory farms, and the animals raised on these farms may be treated more humanely. If you want to eat animal products, look for meat, cheese, milk, and eggs from these farms.

**Oops!** According to a United Nations report, raising livestock is responsible for 18 percent of greenhouse gases (the gases that are causing climate change) in the atmosphere. That is more than cars, buses, and other forms of transportation.

Eating more plants and fewer animals is a delicious way to save resources.

## "Green" eating on the go

You probably eat many of your meals away from home, either at school or in restaurants. Every meal out is an opportunity to create less litter! Here are some tips:

**08** Take your own mug with you when you buy coffee or tea on the run.

**09** Use reusable containers for lunch. Put them in your backpack after you have eaten, so that you remember to take them home and wash them.

**10** Bringing food from home almost always creates less litter than buying food because of all the packaging stores use. It saves you money, too.

**11** Are you going to that restaurant that serves huge portions? Take your own container along, so you can bring the leftovers home with you.

Reusable containers help make lunchtime Earth-friendly.

## Break it down! Composting basics

Instead of tossing fruit and vegetable scraps into the trash can, **compost** them! Materials such as garden waste and food scraps break down over time. Gradually they turn into a rich, dark substance called **humus**, which is part of soil. When the humus is added to a garden, it makes the soil healthier.

### Composting idea 1

A compost pile: This is the simplest way to compost. You just put garden waste in a pile in your garden. If you turn the compost to mix up the pile, you can add food scraps, too. If you don't turn the compost, the food may attract pests.

### Composting idea 2

A compost bin: You use a container to hold the compost. The container can be simply some fencing or mesh formed into a circle or square. Or you can buy a compost bin at a garden center. Some bins rotate, allowing you to turn the compost without using a garden fork.

### Composting idea 3

A wormery: Worms are amazing composters! Put red worms in a special container, along with bedding material, such as shredded newspaper, along with your food scraps. Before long, the worms make a rich compost that is great for gardens. You can order red worms online, or if you live in the country you may be able to get them from a local farmer.

## More ways to eat "green" when you are out

**12** Do you really need to use a big pile of 20 napkins? Only take what you need.

**13** Pack reusable eating utensils with your school lunch so you don't have to use disposable plastic ones.

**14** If you take snacks to school in a plastic bag, take the bag home and reuse it.

**15** Do you really need that plastic lid on your soda, tea, or coffee? If you are walking around while you are drinking it, by all means get one. But if you are just going to sit in a restaurant, you probably don't need it.

**16** Better yet, if you are staying in the restaurant, ask for a real cup rather than a plastic or paper one.

**17** Use cloth napkins. Tuck one into your backpack or keep it in your locker. Remember to take it home to wash it once in a while!

**18** Unless you are in a country where the water is unsafe to drink, try not to buy bottled water. It creates more waste. Tap water will quench your thirst just as effectively.

### Bottled water: Think before you drink

People buy bottled water for a lot of reasons. They may think it is healthier or more convenient, or perhaps they think it looks cool to be seen carrying a famous brand of bottled water.

Bottled water can cost thousands of times more than tap water. So, surely the water inside must be better for you than water straight from the faucet? Wrong! In fact, in some places the rules about what can go into bottled water are weaker than the rules for tap water.

Bottled water is creating a huge plastic waste problem. Worldwide, over 2.5 million tons of plastic are used each year to bottle water. Most water bottles never get recycled. Even if they do, plastic recycling is not as efficient as glass or metal recycling.

There's a simple solution: buy a stainless steel water bottle and fill it from the faucet. The bottles come in different sizes and colors, so you can pick one that suits your personality. The important thing is that you are keeping a lot of plastic bottles out of **landfill** sites.

When you work out, help the planet get healthy, too. Use a stainless steel water bottle.

# Green Glamour

You now know that what you eat and what you drink can help the planet. So can what you wear.

Most clothes you buy are:

- manufactured (which uses energy and creates waste)
- shipped to stores and warehouses (which uses energy and creates pollution and waste)
- sold in stores (which uses energy and creates pollution if you use a car or bus to get there); OR
- ordered online and shipped to your home (which uses energy and creates pollution and waste).

Notice a pattern here? The next time you are desperate to buy yet another striped sweater, think about the energy involved in making the clothes and getting them to you.

Moreover, manufacturing clothes can be pretty tough on the planet. Polyester fabric is made from fossil fuels. Cotton is a natural fiber, but some cotton growers use a lot of chemicals on their crops. Petroleum, a fossil fuel, is used to make many fabric dyes.

Fortunately, there are ways to dress that have less impact on the planet, but look just as good.

Laura Bailey is a model who supports eco-fashion—that is, clothes that are produced in a way that has as little impact on Earth as possible.

Don't toss out the clothes you are tired of. How about swapping them with your friends instead?

**19** Sick of your clothes? Don't throw them out! Have a clothes-exchange party with your friends instead. Donate any leftovers to charity stores.

**20** Instead of buying new clothes, search the racks in charity stores for cool retro fashions and quirky accessories. It is like a treasure hunt—you never know when you will uncover an amazing vintage find.

**21** Learn to knit. (Yes, boys can knit, too!) Unravel those old sweaters full of holes, and knit the wool into funky hats and long scarves for yourself and your friends.

**22** Teach yourself to sew and be your own fashion designer! If you have access to a sewing machine, you can chop, hack, and stitch your boring old clothes and transform them into something original and special. There are books and magazines out there to help you with ideas.

**23** Look around art fairs for unique and affordable clothes and accessories that have been made by local designers or craftspeople. Keep an eye open for fabulous, eco-friendly fabrics, such as organic cotton and hemp.

### Fabulous fabric 1: Bamboo

If you think bamboo is only food for pandas, think again! Bamboo can be turned into chopping boards, kitchen worktops, and clothes. Fabric made from bamboo is light and strong. Best of all, bamboo grows quickly and can be grown without pesticides. So buying and wearing bamboo clothes is a smart environmental move.

### Fabulous fabric 2: Spun plastic

Could you wear an old plastic bottle? Yes, old bottles made from PET (a type of plastic) can be turned into fiber strands, then woven into fabric. The fabric can be made into cozy fleece garments, blankets, and even carpets.

## Oops!

Cotton is another fabulous fabric. After all, where would we be without our jeans? But by some estimates, more than 10 percent of the world's pesticides and 25 percent of its **insecticides** are dumped on cotton crops. These pesticides can harm our soil and water, not to mention the people who work in or live near cotton fields.

However, you don't have to give up on this wonderful fabric. Many farmers are now growing organic cotton, which is much easier on the planet. So when you are shopping for clothes, look for organic cotton on labels.

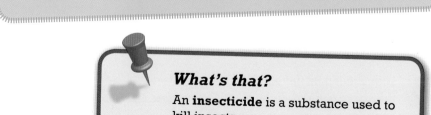

### What's that?
An **insecticide** is a substance used to kill insects.

**24** Reduce clothes washing. Okay, if you have just played a muddy game of soccer, your clothes are probably genuinely dirty. But what about that shirt you wore for only 45 minutes today? Don't toss it in the laundry basket. Put it back in the dresser.

**25** Only use the washing machine when you have a full load of clothes. Always try to wash clothes on a low temperature setting—for example, 30 °C (86 °F). This saves the energy that would have been used to heat the water.

**26** Some kinds of dry cleaning can be bad for the air and for your health. Many dry cleaners use a chemical called perchloroethylene that pollutes the air. One test showed that wearing dry-cleaned clothes just once a week can be a health risk. Luckily, some cleaners are now using **carbon dioxide** to clean clothes instead. Look for one of these eco-friendly cleaners if you have clothes that need to be dry-cleaned.

**listen up!**

You might use makeup. You definitely use soap. Keep an eye open for toiletries and cosmetics with little or no packaging. See if you can find bars of soap or shampoo that are sold without packaging. Some toiletry and cosmetic companies run a refill program for their liquid products, such as shampoo and lotions. Use it! Also, look for products in recyclable metal cans, not plastic tubes.

# Tackle That Trash

You toss an old envelope into the trash can, or throw a plastic bag away. You never see it again. So what's the problem?

The problem is that our trash doesn't magically disappear. It goes somewhere, even if we can't see it anymore. The more of us there are on the planet, the more trash we produce. Our litter affects the lives of humans and other animals—and not in good ways.

Millions of tons of waste are added to landfill sites around the world every year.

Recycling is a good start to helping the planet. It turns old stuff into new stuff, and it helps keep things out of landfill sites. But recycling isn't perfect. It uses energy. And some things can't be recycled easily, or at all.

That's where the "three R's"—*reduce, reuse, recycle*—come in. Recycling stuff is good. Reusing stuff is better. Reducing the amount of stuff you buy in the first place is best of all.

**27** Be a detective. Take a look in the trash cans in your house. How much stuff in there could be composted or recycled? Look at what you are throwing away and figure out the best ways to reduce your total amount of trash in the future.

**28** When you go shopping with your family, take your own bags. It doesn't matter if they are reused plastic bags or cloth bags. The point is to avoid getting a new bag. If you buy something you can carry easily, say "no, thank you" to a bag if the cashier offers you one.

**29** When you open your mailbox, do unwanted catalogs fall out? If they do, here is your good deed for the day: call the toll-free number on each catalog and ask the company to remove your address from its mailing list. (Check with your parents first to make sure it is okay to do this.)

Make your shopping trip Earth-friendly by taking along your own reusable bag.

### Eco-activity: Trash test

Just for one day, make a list of everything you throw out or recycle. At the end of the day, look at your list. Are you surprised? After you have read this book, do the exercise again. Have you made changes that mean you are throwing away less stuff? Why not challenge a friend to a "trash-test": make lists on the same day and see who generates the least trash and recycling. The loser can take the winner out for an eco-friendly treat!

# Oops!

"Downcycling" sounds like cycling down a hill. But it is what some people call plastic recycling. The glass bottles you recycle can be melted down and made into more bottles. A recycled aluminum can may become another aluminum can. This can happen over and over again.

But most of the time when plastic is recycled, it loses quality. It can be recycled a limited number of times. Moreover, most plastic is made from **non-renewable** fuels such as natural gas or oil.

Recycle plastic bottles if you can. Better yet, don't buy them in the first place.

 **Q** Why should you recycle?

 **A** Recycling some things saves a lot of energy. By some estimates, making a drink can from recycled aluminum saves 95 percent of the energy that it would take to make the can from aluminum ore. Even though recycling plastic isn't the most efficient process in the world, it still keeps plastic out of our landfill sites, which are filling up fast.

**Q** Doesn't my trash break down in the landfill site?

**A** Maybe, maybe not. Some things, such as plastic bags, stick around for a long time, possibly hundreds of years. Also, even banana peels and paper need oxygen in order to **decompose**. In some landfill sites, things are packed tightly on top of each other, and some landfills are sealed. In either case, if oxygen can't reach the waste material, the trash can't break down.

**30** Recycle paper. This goes without saying. Put paper in the recycling bin, not the trash can.

**31** Instead of recycling paper with one blank side, reuse it. You may be able to print on the blank side. Or stack the papers blank-side-up and make notepads. Once both sides are used, then recycle it.

**32** Don't drop litter. No one likes wading through trash while walking down the street.

**33** Donate old toys and clothes to a good charity. You will be helping other people and cutting down on waste.

**34** Some waste is very **toxic**. The mercury in thermometers is poisonous and has a poisonous vapor. If you break a thermometer, don't try to clean it up yourself. Tell an adult immediately.

**listen up!**

You are in a public bathroom. You've washed your hands. Your hands are wet. Do you really need to dry them with a paper towel or an electric dryer? Really? Might we suggest you join the Dry-Your-Hands-on-Your-Pants Club? All you need to do to join is dry your hands on your pants. Or shake them dry. Think how much paper would be saved if everyone did this! Granted, you won't want to do this all the time—when you're wearing an evening gown or tuxedo, for example. But most of the time, skipping the towel works just fine. Give it a try!

**35** Recycle your batteries. This is an important one. Batteries contain poisons that can leak into the soil. Take your used batteries to a place that can recycle them. Better still, buy rechargeable batteries.

**36** Recycle your old cell phone. Cell phones don't just take up space in landfills. They also contain toxic substances. Some places will pay cash for your old phone. Others take your phone and give it to someone who needs it.

**37** Instead of buying a CD in a box, purchase MP3 files of the music you want. This will also save on potential plastic recycling. (Remember, you must pay for most music you download, or you will find yourself on the wrong side of the law and may end up with a hefty fine.)

So you have recycled your paper. A company has turned that paper into a recycled-paper product, such as a pad of writing paper or a package of holiday cards. What's next? Someone needs to buy the recycled-paper product! If companies can't sell recycled products, they will lose interest in making them. So when you have a choice, try to buy recycled products.

**listen up!**

## Green giving

**38** Get creative when you are wrapping gifts. Instead of buying expensive wrapping paper, try using old wallpaper samples, or even newspaper tied up with bright fabric strips. You could also use a pretty scarf or a napkin. You could even make a reusable gift bag from fabric.

If you use unusual materials to wrap presents, you can make them unique and special, as well as "green."

Do you have a friend who loves animals? You could make a donation in his or her name to an animal sanctuary.

**39** Give time, not stuff. Instead of giving a material present that will end up in a landfill site, give the gift of your time. Make a certificate saying you will babysit or help with some gardening.

**40** Bake your own presents. Cakes, cookies, and breads make wonderful gifts for most people. And they won't end up in a landfill like that plastic toy you nearly bought.

**41** Give an experience. Is your friend dying to see a particular movie or concert? Tickets would make a great present. Or offer to take your friend on an eco-friendly picnic.

**42** Give a manatee or a pig! Some animal sanctuaries will let you "adopt" an animal, giving you a photo of the animal your money is helping. Any donation will give the satisfaction of helping an animal.

**43** Give a donation in your friend's name to another type of charity. Is your friend concerned about world hunger, or saving rain forests, or rescuing dogs and cats? There is a charity for nearly every concern. (See page 54 for some suggestions, and look online for others.)

# Make Your School Earth-Friendly

You probably spend a lot of time at school. A lot of what you buy is probably for school, too—paper, pens, notebooks, and so on. So school is a terrific opportunity to take planet-friendly action.

Take a look around your school with your new, improved eco-eyes. Are the trash cans full of paper that could be recycled? Are the trash cans in the cafeteria full of wasted food? Do lights get left on in classrooms when no one is inside?

Do you have any suggestions about how your school can become more Earth-friendly? Great! The next step is to get your ideas to the people who can change things. Suggest to your teacher that growing a vegetable garden would be a great class project. If your school has a student council, why not run for it and share your ideas with others? Here are some tips:

**44** Save some wood by buying recycled pencils. You can get pencils made from recycled newspapers, recycled jeans—even recycled money!

**45** Buy refillable pens instead of disposable plastic pens.

**46** Work with your teachers to organize a litter-free day, or a litter-free lunch day at school. Ask the school janitor how many bags of litter your school makes on a normal day. Compare that with the litter-free day.

**47** A lot of college cafeterias are going tray-free to save water. One study showed that washing a single tray takes 1.25 to 1.9 liters (about one-third to one-half gallon) of water. Multiply that by the number of lunches your cafeteria serves each year, and see how much water could be saved! One university saved 11,350 liters (3,000 gallons) of water each day by going tray-less.

**48** Ask what happens to leftover food from the cafeteria. Is it thrown away? If it is, find out if there is a way the food could be donated to feed homeless people instead.

Planting a class vegetable garden is a fun project that everyone can get involved in.

**listen up!**

Part of what makes school fun are activities such as sporting events and dances. If you are helping to organize an event, think about ways to make it easier on the planet.

Serve veggie hotdogs instead of factory-farmed meat. Ask people to bring their own plates, cups, and utensils. Put out bins for waste that can be recycled or composted, in addition to trash cans. If there is an admissions charge, offer a discount for people who walk, cycle, or take public transportation to your event.

## Being green: A class act

**49** Harness the brainpower of other kids in your school. Have a contest for the best eco-friendly school ideas. Each class can come up with something, or individuals can compete against each other. You will end up with a lot of great ideas that your school can consider doing.

**50** Once your school has come up with some great environmental ideas, ask your principal if you can share them with another school in your area. Perhaps that school will have some ideas for your school to use, too!

**51** You know how much paper flies around at school: handouts, tests, homework, notes to your parents, notes from your parents, and so on. Find out if your school uses recycled paper. If it doesn't, suggest that it does. Even if that doesn't work, you can still take charge of your own paper use by buying recycled paper and notebooks, and wasting as little paper as you can.

**52** Make recycling bins for your classroom. Get creative! Can you make them from used cardboard, or from something else that would otherwise be recycled or thrown out? Once the bins are ready, make sure there is a company that collects your school's recycling. If there isn't, talk to your teacher. Perhaps arranging for collection of your school's recyclables would be another good class project!

**listen up!**

Environmental awareness is big business these days. It is so big that some companies stretch the truth about just how eco-friendly they really are. This is called "greenwashing."

For example, a company that makes dangerous pesticides might brag about how its bottles are made from recycled plastic. Well, the bottle part is great, but it is not exactly an Earth-friendly product if it is still full of poisons that end up in the air or water!

Start a class discussion about greenwashing. Take a look at some products that claim to be "green" and discuss whether you think they really are or are not.

It is important to recycle whenever you can. Recycling helps to save resources.

## Super-"green" schools

A lot of school buildings are getting "green" makeovers! At Carver Center School in Midland, Texas, rainwater that falls on the roof is collected and stored in two big tanks. Some of the water is used for the school garden.

# Be Water-Wise

Every living thing, from a potted plant to a person, needs water to survive. If you look at the picture of Earth below, there seems to be water almost everywhere. Oceans and seas cover over 70 percent of Earth's surface. There is even more water in streams, rivers, lakes, and glaciers. So is water one resource we don't need to worry about conserving (saving)?

No! Although we live on a watery planet, nearly all of Earth's water (over 97 percent) is saltwater that we cannot drink. Another 2 percent is frozen in glaciers and polar ice caps. So less than 1 percent of Earth's water is available for our use. We need to do two things: save water, and keep the water we have clean.

Earth's oceans are full of saltwater, but drinkable water is a rare resource.

**53** Turn off the faucet while you are brushing your teeth, instead of letting the water run. Assuming you brush your teeth twice a day, this will save about 30 liters (6.5 gallons) of water a day.

**54** Check your faucets at home for leaks. Put a few drops of food coloring in your toilet cistern and don't flush the toilet for at least 15 minutes. If you see colored water in the toilet bowl, you know there is a leak. If you notice a dripping faucet when you are out, tell the management.

**55** Take shorter showers. This is another easy way to make a big difference every single day.

**56** Don't use the toilet to dispose of tissues. Drop tissues in the trash can instead. There is no need to waste water every time you use a tissue.

Don't let clean water flow down the drain. Turn off the faucet while you brush.

# Quiz

## Test your water IQ

a) How much water does a full bath use?

b) How much water does a five-minute shower use?

c) How much water does the average person in the United States use daily?

**Find out the truth!**

a) 265 liters (70 gallons)
b) 38-95 liters (10-25 gallons)
c) More than 99 gallons (375 liters) per day

## Go with the low-flow

Many homes and businesses have low-flow faucets and showerheads. Less water comes out, but they work just as well. There are also toilets with two different flushes: the one for solid waste uses more water than the one for liquid waste. If your family is renovating a kitchen or bathroom, suggest that the adults consider low-flow fixtures.

**57** Are you fond of cold, refreshing glasses of water? Keep a jug of water in the refrigerator instead of letting the faucet run until it is cold.

**58** Put the stopper in the bathtub before you turn on the water for your bath.

**59** Instead of using the hose to clean your patio, sidewalk, or driveway, sweep them with a broom.

true story

## Planet hero: Ryan Hreljac

When Ryan Hreljac was six years old, he learned that people in Africa were dying because they did not have clean water. Ryan wanted to do something about it. He managed to raise some money and used it to build a well in Uganda. Ryan didn't stop there. Today, the Ryan's Well Foundation is responsible for getting clean water to over half a million people. If a six-year-old can start something this big, think about what *you* can do!

**60** Wash the family car or your bike with water in a bucket, instead of turning on a hose and letting it run. Better still, find a car wash that recycles the water it uses. Remember, any detergent you use to wash the car at home may end up in lakes or the ocean.

**61** Don't let water run while you wash the dishes. If you have two sinks, fill up one with washing water and one with rinsing water.

# Oops!

The Great Pacific Garbage Patch is a huge mass of waste floating in the Pacific Ocean. It is made up of a lot of pieces of plastic. One study found that the Garbage Patch averages over half a million pieces of plastic per square mile. It is thought by some to cover an area bigger than Texas, while others estimate it to be the size of the continental United States.

Our plastic waste is causing big problems for the ocean and the animals that live in it. Animals can die when they eat the plastic, or when they get tangled up in it. One study estimated that over 40,000 northern fur seals in the Bering Sea die every year when they get tangled in plastic. And that is just one species, and one location.

## Fishy issues

People used to think that they could catch as many fish as they wanted, because the sea would always have enough. Now we know that isn't true. **Overfishing** has become a big problem.

Why? Well, these days fishing is no longer done by small groups of people with modest-sized nets or fishing rods. Now huge boats can catch tons of fish with a single scoop of their enormous nets.

When fish are scooped up, other animals get trapped in the big nets as well. These animals, called by-catch, also die. Dolphins, sea turtles, and seals are all animals that get killed as by-catch.

### Farming fish

Some people have begun raising fish on fish farms. Oyster and clam farms do not cause much damage to the environment. But some fish, like salmon, are raised in net pens in the ocean. If fish are crowded together, disease can spread easily from one fish to another. And since lots of fish means lots of fish waste, the farms can pollute the ocean.

### What's that?

**Overfishing** means taking too many fish from one area.

Some farmed fish are raised in tanks, but others live in large cages by the sea.

## More ways to keep water clean

**62** If you notice that the family car is leaking oil, tell an adult. Oil on the ground gets washed down drains, and then into lakes, rivers, and the sea. Just a few liters of engine oil can pollute millions of liters of water.

**63** Use safer cleaning products. You can scrub a sink with baking soda or polish furniture with beeswax. A mix of vinegar and water in a spray bottle makes a great glass cleaner.

**64** Reduce pesticide use in the garden. You can make sprays that kill certain pests by mixing water with garlic or salt (look online for recipes). Ladybugs like to eat pests called aphids. What would you rather have floating around in your garden: lovely ladybugs or toxic chemicals?

**65** Clean up after pets. Pet waste will pollute water if rainwater carries it into streams and lakes.

Ladybugs will eat
up garden pests.

# Spare the Air

Take a deep breath, then let it out slowly. Ahhh . . . Doesn't that feel good? We wouldn't survive long without fresh air. It gives our bodies the oxygen we need in order to function.

But there is a lot of stuff around that can pollute our air. Air pollution comes from all sorts of places: factories, cars and buses, power plants, cigarettes, and even certain kinds of paints and glues. In some countries, air quality has improved in the last 20 years. This is partly because of tougher laws against pollution. But in other places, the air is getting worse.

We need to protect Earth's air supply. Polluted air is not good for any of the animals on Earth, including humans. Air pollution is even changing the world's climate. So let's start the cleanup!

## Oops!

Acid rain is what you get when pollutants make water in the air more acidic than usual. When the acid rain falls to Earth, it can harm plants and animals. It can even eat away at statues and buildings. Car exhaust fumes and burning fossil fuels contribute to acid rain.

Cycling is a form of transportation and exercise all rolled into one!

**66** Don't smoke. Smoking puts pollution into the air, not to mention into your body. Who needs that?

**67** Try to use public transportation instead of using a car.

**68** Encourage your family to start up a carpool with friends. It saves fuel and makes the journey more fun!

**69** Cycle or walk to school. If it is too far, ask whoever drives you to drop you off about a mile away from school (if it is safe). You'll get some great exercise and save a little gasoline.

This velomobile will keep your homework dry in the rain. Your head sticks out, but the rest of your body is inside!

**listen up!**

Sometimes there is an all-too-familiar problem with riding your bike. It's called rain! Arriving at school a soggy, dripping mess doesn't exactly get your day off to a great start. That's where the velomobile comes in. A velomobile is an environmentally friendly pedal-powered car that is enclosed (so no problem with raindrops making your lunch soggy). There are not many on the road at the moment, but who knows? As people look for ways to stop climate change, pedal cars may become the next big thing.

## Changing climate

Why is Earth heating up? It is partly because of something called the enhanced greenhouse effect. Greenhouses are great places to grow plants. They trap heat from the Sun, so the temperature inside the greenhouse is warmer than the temperature outside.

Certain gases, such as carbon dioxide, surround Earth and trap the Sun's heat like the glass walls of a greenhouse. Without this greenhouse effect, Earth would be so cold that we couldn't survive. When we burn fossil fuels, however, more greenhouse gases are released into the air. These extra gases are making Earth's temperature rise.

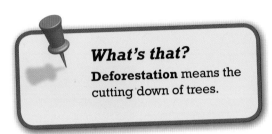

**What's that?**
**Deforestation** means the cutting down of trees.

**Deforestation** adds to the problem. Trees store carbon dioxide. Burning a tree releases carbon dioxide, a greenhouse gas, into the atmosphere. Plus the tree is no longer around to pull carbon dioxide from the air.

**70** Plant a tree. Ask if you can plant one in your yard, or ask your teacher if your class can plant some trees in your neighborhood as a class project.

**71** Get a houseplant. Even a small plant can get rid of carbon dioxide and toxins. Spider plants and gerbera daisies are good choices. If you have pets, make sure the plants you buy are not toxic to animals.

**72** If you celebrate Christmas, get a living Christmas tree. After the holidays, you can plant it outside. And you will save a tree from being cut down.

Plants are not just nice to look at—they are also natural air cleaners! They use carbon dioxide and light from the Sun to make food and oxygen. They can even filter toxic chemicals out of the air.

**listen up!**

**73** If you buy a cut Christmas tree, see if you can recycle it. Some local governments will pick up old trees, or you can compost it with your garden waste.

**74** Learn about the world's rain forests. These lush tropical forests found near Earth's equator make a lot of our oxygen and use up a lot of carbon dioxide. They are also home to thousands of different kinds of animals. Do some rain forest research and find out about ways you can help protect these important forests.

Plants make oxygen, and they are nice to look at, too. Why not have a planting party with your friends?

**true story**

# Planet hero: Wangari Maathai

Wangari Maathai is a Kenyan woman who started the Green Belt Movement, an organization that helps people and the environment. The Green Belt Movement has over 600 community networks in Kenya. It is responsible for the planting of over 30 million trees!

# Conserving Power

You walk into your kitchen, flip a switch, and the lights come on. You open the refrigerator and take out some juice. It's cold. You press a button and your computer comes on. Whether it is electrical power, natural gas power, or another type, we rely on power every day.

Have you ever thought about where your electricity comes from? Okay, we know about the socket in the wall! But before electrical power travels to your home or school, it needs to be produced.

Some electricity is made with the energy from flowing water. **Nuclear power** plants make some electricity. But most electricity in the United States is produced by factories that burn fossils fuels, such as coal. Earth has a limited supply of fossil fuels. They are non-renewable. Eventually, we are going to run out of them.

So how can you help cut down on fossil fuel use? By conserving power! Fortunately, there are a lot of easy ways to do that. Sometimes all you need to do is flip a switch!

**Q** Do fossil fuels really come from fossils?

**A** Yes! Fossil fuels such as oil, natural gas, and coal formed from plants and animals that lived millions of years ago. When they died, their bodies broke down and were covered by sand, rock, and mud. Over time, they turned into fossil fuels. The plants and animals in most of our fossil fuels lived at least 300 million years ago. That's before dinosaurs roamed Earth.

Here's a bright idea: use compact fluorescent lightbulbs!

**75** Install compact fluorescent lightbulbs (CFLs). They use much less power than standard, incandescent bulbs. An incandescent bulb uses four times as much power to produce the same amount of light as a CFL. CFLs last a lot longer, too.

**76** Turn off the lights! If you're not hanging out in a room, flip the switch.

**77** Keep your refrigerator and freezer full. That way, they use less energy. A good way to fill up is to fill plastic jugs with water and put them in the refrigerator.

**78** Do you feel a *whoosh* of cool air when you open the refrigerator? For all the cold air that's whooshing out, there is an equal amount of warm air whooshing in. It needs to be cooled down, which takes energy. Decide what you want before opening the refrigerator door, and don't open it more than you need to.

## Eco-exercise: Have an unpowered hour!

When was the last time you and your family sat around together in the dark without the television on? Pick an hour when everyone's at home and agree not to use any power: no television, no computers, no lights. You can light some candles, play a board game, maybe even talk to each other! You might like it so much that you choose to have an unpowered hour every week.

You don't need all the lights on to relax and have fun.

## Renewable energy

It is likely that we will run out of fossil fuels one day. Luckily, there are also **renewable** energy sources. For instance, solar (Sun) energy is renewable, because we're not going to run out of power from the Sun. Power made by water and wind is also renewable. So is power made from plants.

However, just because energy is renewable, that does not necessarily mean it is good. Burning wood to heat your home uses a renewable resource, but it also pollutes the air. To keep Earth healthy, we are going to need energy sources that are both renewable *and* **sustainable**.

**What's that?**
**Sustainable** means something that doesn't harm Earth and won't run out, such as sunlight that can provide solar power.

**79** Items such as computers use a little bit of energy from the socket even when they are turned off. If you are going on vacation, unplug your computer, television, and other electrical appliances.

**80** Get a solar-powered calculator.

**81** Put a lid on it! If you are boiling a pot of water, cover it with a lid to prevent heat from escaping. This will make it heat up faster.

**82** Shut down your computer at night.

**83** Microwave ovens can use less than half the energy of standard ovens, so microwaving a meal can be energy-smart.

**84** Suggest to your family that you keep your home a little cooler in the winter by setting the central heating at a lower temperature. Put on a warm sweater and socks if you're cold. In the summer, don't set the air conditioning at too cold a temperature. Just a few degrees can save a lot of energy.

### Fossil fuel in . . . a box of crayons?

What do car and bike tires, crayons, and plastic have in common? Believe it or not, they are all made from petroleum, a fossil fuel. Fossil fuels lurk in a lot of everyday products. By using less stuff, you can help conserve fossil fuels.

# Give Animals a Helping Hand

Sometimes humans behave as though we are the only animals on Earth. But the fact is we share our planet with millions of other species. When we pollute the water or the air or destroy habitats, it affects other animals.

One big problem for animals is habitat destruction. For example, lemurs are fascinating creatures that live only on the islands of Madagascar and Comoro, near Africa. Unfortunately, their forest homes are being cut down for **logging** and development. Many species of lemurs are already classified as **endangered species**.

Since humans are responsible for these changes, we should give our fellow animals a helping hand when we can. Even small things you do can make life easier for our furry, feathered, and scaly animal friends.

**listen up!**

Climate change is affecting all the animals on Earth, even polar bears who live way up in the Arctic. Because the planet is warming, the ice on which the bears live is melting away. As the ice melts, the bears can get stranded on floating blocks of ice, unable to reach safety.

**85** Don't flush cat waste down the toilet. It can carry organisms that make sea otters and other marine creatures sick. If you flush it away, the organisms can end up in the sea.

**86** Snip the rings on plastic six-pack holders before you throw them away. Fish and birds can get caught in the rings and choke.

**87** That balloon drifting across the sky is going to end up somewhere, perhaps in the sea. Animals such as sea turtles can mistake balloons for jellyfish, eat them, and then die. So save animals by hanging on to your balloons.

**88** Keep an eye open for plastic bags on the street and pick them up. Like balloons, plastic bags can kill animals that mistake them for food and eat them.

**89** If your family wants a pet, adopt an animal from a local shelter. There are always plenty of great pets that need homes. Millions of animals are killed each year because there are not enough homes for them. By saving a pet from a shelter, you are helping to stop this problem. Once you get your pet, be sure to have it spayed or neutered.

**90** Cats roaming around outside are a nightmare for wild birds. If you have a cat, consider keeping it inside. This will keep your pet safe from other animals and cars, too. If you want your cat to roam free, a bell on the collar will give birds some warning so they can get away.

**91** If you see someone mistreating an animal, tell an adult immediately.

**92** As there are more people on the planet, there are fewer wild places left for animals to live. Raise money to donate to a group that protects animal habitats. Keep a corner of your yard wild to provide homes for butterflies and insects.

**93** Get wise about animals, even ones that seem creepy or scary. For example, bats may look frightening. But one bat can eat 3,000 mosquitoes in one night! Sharks also seem frightening. But predators such as sharks help to keep the oceans healthy. The more you know about how cool animals are, the more you will want to protect them.

**94** If you see an injured wild animal, call the ASPCA or your local wildlife rescue organization. They can tell you what to do to help it.

**95** Never release a domestic animal into the wild. It may not be able to take care of itself, and it may cause problems for the animals that actually belong there.

true story

## Planet hero: Jane Goodall

When Jane Goodall was 23 years old, she traveled from the United Kingdom to Tanzania to study wild chimpanzees. Her work with chimpanzees made her famous, and also helped her understand that human activities such as logging are putting animals in danger. In 1991 Jane Goodall and 16 young people founded the Roots & Shoots program. This program encourages kids to do things to help people, animals, and the environment. Today, there are tens of thousands of Roots & Shoots members in nearly 100 countries.

# Quiz

## What is a dead zone?

a) a part of the ocean with so little oxygen that animals can't survive

b) a place where vampires and zombies hang out and party

c) a cemetery.

### Find out the truth!

The answer is a. Dead zones are largely the result of the use of **fertilizers**, substances people use to help grow their crops. The fertilizers get washed into the oceans, where they make huge amounts of **algae** grow. When the algae die, they decompose. This process uses up the oxygen in the water.

## It's all connected

By now you have probably figured out that practically everything in this book is connected in some way. This means that one little thing you do can help Earth and its animals in a lot of ways!

- If you cycle instead of drive, you help keep the air clean AND you reduce the greenhouse gases that are heating up the polar bears' Arctic homes.
- If you reuse your shopping bag, you save resources AND you keep plastic out of the environment where an animal might eat it.
- If you eat low on the food chain, you cut down on pollution AND you save water AND you discourage factory farming.

So remember, even a single action can have a big impact!

# Get Active

Congratulations! You are now a walking encyclopedia, full of knowledge about how to help the planet. You know how to eat and dress "green." You know how to save energy, save water, and keep litter out of the environment. You know how to help animals, and how to make your school a more Earth-friendly place.

So what's left for an eco-genius like you to do? Take action! That includes reaching out to others to help make them as eco-aware as you are. If one person can do a lot, think of how much more a group can do!

Do you have a great idea about how you and some friends can make your town more environmentally friendly? Is there one environmental issue that you are very concerned about? Write a letter, raise some money, put up a website—there are countless ways you can help!

A park cleanup day is a fun way to help the planet and hang out with your friends.

**96** Is there too much litter in a park or street near you? Get an adult's help and organize a cleanup. Have a pizza party afterward to celebrate.

**97** When you visit a park or wildlife reserve, respect the plant life and animal life. Don't pick the plants, and don't do anything to annoy the animals. (You wouldn't want someone coming into your home and annoying you!)

**98** Have a garage sale or a bake sale to raise money for an environmental charity, such as Greenpeace or Rainforest Action Network.

**99** Write a letter to the president or your local representatives in Congress saying how important it is that adults work to protect the environment. After all, kids can't do it all alone!

**100** Write a play with your friends about a chosen environmental issue. Perform it for some younger kids.

Car washing for friends and neighbors is a good way to raise money for an environmental charity. Just make sure you use a bucket instead of a hose, to save water.

**true story**

## Planet hero: Alec Loorz

When Alec Loorz was 12, he saw the movie *An Inconvenient Truth*, which describes the threat of climate change. Alec wanted to do something to help, so in 2007 he founded Kids vs. Global Warming. The group educates other young people about climate change. Alec, who gives presentations to people of all ages, has won many awards for his work. He says:

"Lots of kids feel that they really can't make a difference. But I know that our voice matters more than anyone else's. We are the ones who will be most affected by what the world does or doesn't do NOW to change the way we use fossil fuels."

## How to write a good letter

Want to make your voice heard? Writing a letter is a good way to start. You could send an email instead. But since writing an actual letter on paper takes more effort, letters tend to get more attention from decision-makers than emails.

Here are some letter-writing tips:

- Decide who should get your letter. If it is a local issue, you might want to write to your local government. If it is a national issue, you could write to your local representatives in Congress.
- Put your own address and date at the top of the letter.
- Find out what address to send the letter to. You can do this online. This address comes afer the date.
- Use the right greeting. "Dear Senator" definitely won't work! Find out the person's name. Again, you can search online for this.
- In your letter, briefly say who you are and what you would like the person to do. Be polite!
- Check your spelling carefully, and make the letter as neat as you can. Write neatly, or type it on the computer and print it out.
- End with a polite closing, such as "Yours sincerely, (your name)" or "Yours truly, (your name)."
- Write out the envelope neatly, put on a stamp, and put it in the mailbox!

**101** Spread the word to, and set a good example for, younger children. It is hard to believe, but that little kid next door might be president one day. Now that you are an expert about saving Earth, pass on some of your knowledge to younger kids. If you see them littering or wasting water, explain to them why they shouldn't. But be nice— no one likes getting lectured to or yelled at. If you have a younger brother or sister, perhaps he or she can help you do some of the things in this book. Our Earth needs all the help it can get!

Now that you are an eco-genius, share your knowledge with others to help the planet and save the natural world.

"Nature is the original punk. Eco can be edgy, loud, fun, playful . . . and hyper-cool. What's your punk?"

Linda Loudermilk, eco-fashion designer

# Glossary

**acid rain** rain that has a higher-than-usual level of acid in it because of pollution

**algae** tiny plant-like organisms

**carbon dioxide** gas found in the air. Plants use it when making food, and both plants and animals give it off when they breathe.

**compost** mixture of decomposing plants that can be used to enrich soil. Also, the act of making material into compost.

**decompose** break down or rot

**deforestation** cutting down trees

**endangered species** group of animals at risk of dying out

**environment** everything that surrounds a living thing

**fertilizer** substance that people use to help crops grow

**fossil fuel** material such as oil, coal, and natural gas that formed within Earth from plants and animals that lived millions of years ago

**habitat** place where an organism, such as an animal, lives

**humus** dark substance in soil that nourishes plants

**insecticide** substance used to kill insects

**landfill** disposal of waste by burying it

**logging** chopping down trees to be used as timber

**non-renewable** something, such as a natural resource, that cannot be replaced

**nuclear power** energy produced by splitting the atoms of certain materials

**organic** food grown without using artificial chemicals

**overfishing** taking too many fish from an area of the ocean

**pesticide** substance used to kill a pest

**renewable** something, such as a natural resource, that Earth cannot run out of

**resource** substance that is available for use

**sustainable** something, such as a natural resource, that Earth cannot run out of and that will not damage Earth

**toxic** poisonous

# Find Out More

## Books

Gore, Al. *An Inconvenient Truth: The Planetary Emergency of Global Warming and What We Can Do About It*. New York: Rodale, 2006.

Hegarty, Mark. *The Little Book of Living Green*. Kansas City: Andrews McMeel, 2008.

Montez, Michelle, and Lorraine Bodger. *The New 50 Simple Things Kids Can Do to Save the Earth*. Kansas City: Andrews McMeel, 2009.

Simon, Seymour. *Global Warming*. New York: Collins, 2010.

Todd, Anne Marie. *Life Skills: Get Green!* Chicago: Heinemann Library, 2009.

Townsend, John. *Why Science Matters: Predicting the Effects of Climate Change*. Chicago: Heinemann Library, 2009.

## Websites

**www.greenpeace.org/international/campaigns/oceans**
This section of the Greenpeace website gives you information about by-catch, pollution, and overfishing in the world's oceans.

**www.worldwildlife.org**
The website of the World Wildlife Fund has lots of information about how climate change is affecting animals and their habitats, as well as ways for you to get involved.

**www.greenschools.net**
Visit the website of the Green Schools Initiative, which works to make schools more environmentally friendly.

**www.energysavers.gov**
This U.S. Department of Energy website offers lots of great tips on saving energy.

**www.rootsandshoots.org**
Visit the Roots & Shoots website to find out more about how you can get involved to help people, animals, and the environment around the world.

**www.ryanswell.ca**
Visit this website to find out more about Ryan Hreljac and how he came to set up Ryan's Well Foundation. You'll also find suggestions about how you can get involved in the struggle to bring clean water to people all over the world.

**www.greenbeltmovement.org**
Learn more about Wangari Maathai and the Green Belt Movement on this website. You can also pledge to plant a tree as part of the Billion Tree Campaign.

**http://kids-vs-global-warming.com**
Read about why Alec Loorz set up the Kids vs. Global Warming website. Check out the environmental projects his organization is taking part in.

## Topics to research

- When you next visit the supermarket, take a look around at the shelves. Which foods seem to have the most packaging? Which foods have the least? Can you think of ways in which people can reduce the number of packaged foods they buy?

- Many people drive cars rather than cycling, walking, or taking public transportation. What are some reasons for this? Can you think of ways that cycling and taking public transportation can be made easier, safer, and more fun?

- Choose an endangered animal species and learn more about it. Why is the species endangered? Are humans partly or wholly responsible? What steps can people take to help the species recover?

# Index